# THE SOUL'S HOME

*other books by the author*

POETRY
Dawn Visions
Burnt Heart/Ode to the War Dead
This Body of Black Light Gone Through the Diamond
The Desert is the Only Way Out
The Chronicles of Akhira
The Blind Beekeeper
Mars & Beyond
Laughing Buddha Weeping Sufi
Salt Prayers
Ramadan Sonnets
Psalms for the Brokenhearted
I Imagine a Lion
Coattails of the Saint
Abdallah Jones and the Disappearing-Dust Caper (illustrated by the author)
Love is a Letter Burning in a High Wind
The Flame of Transformation Turns to Light
Underwater Galaxies
The Music Space
Cooked Oranges
Through Rose Colored Glasses
Like When You Wave at a Train and the Train Hoots Back at You
In the Realm of Neither
The Fire Eater's Lunchbreak
Millennial Prognostications
You Open a Door and it's a Starry Night
Where Death Goes
Shaking the Quicksilver Pool
The Perfect Orchestra
Sparrow on the Prophet's Tomb
A Maddening Disregard for the Passage of Time
Stretched Out on Amethysts
Invention of the Wheel
Sparks Off the Main Strike
Chants for the Beauty Feast
In Constant Incandescence
Holiday from the Perfect Crime
The Caged Bear Spies the Angel
The Puzzle
Ramadan is Burnished Sunlight
Ala-udeen & The Magic Lamp (illustrated by the author)
The Crown of Creation (illustrated by the author)
Blood Songs
Down at the Deep End (with drawings by the author)
Next Life
A Hundred Little 3D Pictures
He Comes Running (chapbook)
Miracle Songs for the Millennium
The Throne Perpendicular to All that is Horizontal
The Soul's Home

THEATER / THE FLOATING LOTUS MAGIC OPERA COMPANY
The Walls Are Running Blood
Bliss Apocalypse

# THE SOUL'S HOME

poems

February 14 – October 8, 2013

•

Daniel Abdal-Hayy Moore

The Ecstatic Exchange
2014
Philadelphia

The Soul's Home
Copyright © 2014 Daniel Abdal-Hayy Moore
All rights reserved.
Printed in the United States of America

For quotes any longer than those for critical articles and reviews, contact:
*The Ecstatic Exchange,*
6470 Morris Park Road, Philadelphia, PA 19151-2403
email: abdalhayy@danielmoorepoetry.com

First Edition
ISBN: 978-0-578-14224-1 (paper)
Published by *The Ecstatic Exchange,*
6470 Morris Park Road, Philadelphia, PA 19151-2403

Front cover art by Malika Moore, *The Rainbow Bismin*, based on the famous calligraphy by Moroccan Shaykh Muhammad b. Al-Qasim al-Qandusi (died:1861)

Back cover photograph © Lou Wilson

## DEDICATION

To
Shaykh ibn al-Habib
(and the continuation of the Habibiyya)
Shaykh Bawa Muhaiyuddeen,
all shuyukh of instruction and ma'arifa
and
Baji Tayyaba Khanum
of the unsounded depths

*The earth is not bereft
of Light*

## CONTENTS

Author's Introduction   10
Three Pilgrims   13
A Million Birds   16
Heart to Heart   19
Holy Spots   20
The World Looks Very Different   22
Lightning Bolts   24
The Path   26
Songs of Our Souls   32
The Joys of a Breath   35
The Puzzle   37
Perspicacious   40
A Sunset   42
Prostration   43
In Switzerland   44
Along the Way   61
They Let Me Down Slowly   63
The Waters of Night   64
Silver Ladder   66
The Weight of The World   67
Horses of Fajr   69
The Day Comes   70
Single Pointed   71
Touchstone   74
Somebody's Knocking   76
Equipoise   78
Something   81
To Reach the Water   83

Last Day   85
Vanishing Horizon   87
Naked Before My Cat   89
Where the Greatest Wisdom Is   90
Lotus in Reverse   92
We Could Dry Up   94
If I Turned into Death   95
At the Square Edge   97
I Float in a Sea   100
I Get Ready for Sleep   101
A Long Session of Non Sequiturs   103
Water That Trickles   105
Paradise of Buzzes   106
What is Lost   107
Since When Did the World   110
The Certain Gaze the Sky Has   111
Time Goes So Fast   113
Its Silver Threads   115
The Savage in the Lamplight   117
Waking Up in the Same Room   119
Is That His Love?   121
They Say   124
Get Up Out of Sound Sleep   128
Answer Enough   130
God's One Day   132
Snail of Light   134
Leviathan's Sleep   135
Night After Night   136
How Do We Break the Shell Open   138
Death is a Pinhole   140
Hold onto the Little Handles   142

Dog Tired   143
The Sublime   144
When the Door Swings Open   145
Always Perfect   147
God's Glance   148
Uncreated   150
Door   152
Where We Sit Still   153
All the Prophets   154
To Be Lowered Down   156
If it's a Butterfly Poem You Want   158
Not Till   159
One Drop in a Pool   160
We All Have to Die   161
A Strange Hole in Our Being   163
Doubt   165
A Scattering of Ashes   166
The Family of Man   167
Not So Fast!   170
The Particulars of Any Given Thing   171
The Corkscrewing Motion   174
The Great Bear's Back   176
When the Subject is Love   177
I Should Sleep   180
If I Lay My Head   182
Lambs and Lions   184
Poem Found on a Scrap of Paper and Reconsidered   186
From the Soft Rope We Are   187
Death Delights in Our Amorous Play   189
The Sound of Grass Growing   190
From Our Point of View   193

Grizzly Pantomime     196
Nearsightedness    198
Enter from the Right     199
When an Angel Passes by Your Door     201
Death Sits in All Our Windows     202
Drawn to the Presence     204
Bubbles    205
Beauty in the Breath     207
In Honor of All the Poets     209
He's Left This World     211
In a Well    213
Velvet Glove    215
Filled to Overflowing     216

INDEX    220

# AUTHOR'S INTRODUCTION

This collection from 2013 continues the intended trajectory of a lifetime's work that celebrates and posits the direct perception that The Divine Reality faces us from everywhere and in literally every circumstance of each moment of our lives.

In this, the world's soul envelope has been turned inside out, revealing itself in images of light. Rather than invoking metaphors for experience, my project has been to "move from the word as symbol toward the word as reality" (as W.C. Williams said about the poetry of Ezra Pound), words not *standing for* an already completed experience, physical or spiritual, but *in the act of writing itself* revealing the core, the poem's very details being in themselves the experience, between seen and unseen, with transitive imagination the active aesthetic practice, as much as Allah inspires and allows. The poem is itself first-hand, flowering out and echoing its meanings in its very language. To see the world both close and galactic in its radiant divine aspect, in Blake's sense of it, with the Gates of Perception cleansed, our senses and our hearts, now through Sufi practice and revelational theology, open to all.

The French Surrealists developed a language for this, although their project differed, plumbing the "subconscious," with little focus on the divine behind or within it. But in doing this they eschewed metaphor in favor of a kind of things-as-they-are, however irrational or dreamlike, as in Andre Breton's famous:

> My wife with hair of a wood fire
> With thoughts of heat lightning
> With waist of an hourglass
> With waist of an otter in a tiger's teeth…

This demands a different kind of reading, where the reader / listener in suspending disbelief goes with the torrent of imagery to the goal of radiating light, and the poem is more the mirror image of an ever-elusive subject. Certainly the classical Sufi poets are adept at this, those God-inspired surrealists, erasing any differentiations between this world and the next, bringing both into each other's realms for a deeper totality of vision. And as their subject is always Allah, our self's dimishment and ours soul's cosmic expansion, their always-seeking is the process we engage in with them when we read or sing their poems — the true *raison d'etre* of poetry.

So a sometime forced entrance into a more rapt and even rapturous consciousness may be by abruptly strange, even irrational means, an inspiration to begin with juxtapositions of imagery that bypass the conscious mind to deeper chambers of sense. These poems are meant to be a *dhikr*, remembrance of Allah, some circumstantial, some casual, even ephemeral, some with humor, others by Allah with stronger depth-charges seeking richer ore. But always, as "ecstatic exchange" vehicles, between the "I" and annihilation, between articulator and silent worlds, between life itself and death's eventuality, and then needing reader or listener to complete the circle, the final exchange, to fill out the event of the poem with an equally receptive heart — heart-listening being crucial to the process of writing them, and that which fulfills their existence by its completion in others.

As my initial "mission statement" has it, posted years ago at the beginning of the project, *"For me the province of poetry is a private ecstasy made public, and the social role of the poet is to display moments of shared universal epiphanies capable of healing our sense of mortal estrangement — from ourselves, from each other, from our source, from our destiny, from The Divine."*

The One does not aspire to us, to move around us; we aspire to it, to move around it. Actually, we always move around it; but we do not always look. We are like a chorus grouped around a conductor who allow their attention to be distracted by the audience. If, however, they were to turn towards their conductor, they would sing as they should and would really be with him. We are always around The One. If we were not, we would dissolve and cease to exist. Yet our gaze does not remain fixed upon the One. When we look at it, we then attain the end of our desires and find rest. Then it is that, all discord past, we dance an inspired dance around it. In this dance the soul looks upon the source of life, the source of The Intelligence, the origin of Being, the cause of the Good, the root of the Soul.
— Plotinus, Enneads. [Trans: Elmer O'Brien.]


Abu Hasan Shadhili, may Allah be pleased with him, said:
"Whoever directs you to this world has cheated you; whoever directs you to deeds has exhausted you; but whoever directs you to Allah has truly counseled you."
— Al-Ghazali [Trans: T.J.Winter]

You have meanings as the sea has waves
— Shaykh Darqawi (Letter 95 / Trans: Aisha Bewley)

Play wrong and make it right
— Thelonious Monk

## THREE PILGRIMS

Three pilgrims walk along
and each one is

part of the other

"How can you see ahead of us
with your blind eyes?" one

shouts and the other replies
"Your growls are my handlebars"

"How can you saunter with your
game knee?" one cajoles

and the other replies
"You sway from side to side
like a boat

and I flow with it"

"How do you keep up with your
flippity heartbeat?" one yells

and the other replies
"We three hearts make
one normal whizz-bang

and so you complete me"

Clad from head to toe in tatters
these three make a sorry sight

Dogs bark at them
Small boys throw rocks

They are often heard singing
down by the tracks

"Only God creates anyone

We praise Him in the rain
we praise him in the sun

If He takes my arm
I'll use the other one

Don't let calamity unseat you
If you can't walk

like a cuckoo clock
you can still run

Only God creates anyone

We praise Him in the rain
We praise Him in the sun"

They walked along
conscious of the air

these three pilgrims
going somewhere

2/14

## A MILLION BIRDS

A million birds all turn at once
to convince you

A snow flower on a Himalayan peak
opens for ten minutes once a

year its deep purply-yellow velvety golden
petals slimed with gum a particular

butterfly visits that very moment
and sips to produce her eggs

A volcanic air vent at the bottom of the sea
exhaling sulfur brings unaccountable

joy to a family of tube worms
who are the only creatures who can

take the nauseous heat in case you are
bereft of wonder or

overwhelmed with doubt

yet none of these Disneyesque
events might bring the rock-hard

heart to tears

but the skies rent apart with
terrific force and all its curtains

ripped straight down to
show us what indescribable

next-worldly otherworldly twelve-
dimensional consequential revels are

playing on glass tambourines and
nostril calliopes hearts as big as

suns being beaten like gongs and
pancreas drums by femur

drumsticks booming among silver
clouds so sharp they emit sparks

slicing the air into dangling shreds
as God's Mercy pours its endless

slant rays through the threads of each
hallucinatory fabric of every event of ours

to bathe our grateful innermost
faces once and for all

to convince us
more than even the subtlest

thought itself of ours
can convince us

and we can
take a breath among the

truly alive at last

2/16

# HEART TO HEART

I had an interesting talk with my
cardiologist the other day
when I asked him if he ever did
heart surgery

and he said yes but he doesn't do
anything that requires
cutting through bone he
leaves that to his colleagues

and they dispute their respective
approaches where he uses
catheters and they saw through ribs
but end up applying the same
methods he does after all to get the
same results

and I said it must cause some
heated discussions at
cardiologist banquets
and do they ever get into
food fights over it and he said
yes occasionally

but I think he was just joking

2/16

## HOLY SPOTS

They hang around holy spots
the three of them

recent birds' nests births
fatal crashes

God's anointings

and how the earth could have a
silver string run through all the

holes of its holy spots
and worn like a diamond ball

around the neck of a holy one
one or all

three of them
around the single

neck of the three of them

and how out of these holy spots
a glittering incense pours

that has our faces on it
in perfect repose

eyelids heavy with moonlight
and they

dwell in the light of that moonlight
the three of them

and sing to the source spine
of all of us

and our responses are how our
heartbeats recognize

the lit Path all around us
of each moment's compassion

a surgical cut that pulls
death away from the edge

for more time among the living
and the amount of

gratitude we show for it
having come this far

on their way somewhere
the three of them

each one
part of the other one

2/18

# THE WORLD LOOKS VERY DIFFERENT

The world looks very different in the
middle of the night

The planets leaning in slightly sunward
even in pitch dark

and our hearts in suspension if not a blissful
suspension of disbelief

as silver rivers pour through the silence of our
rooms and all the creatures of the

night find their eyes to look out of or
behind those lidded ones to sleep

On an ivory bridge somewhere
carved with filigree and scenes from the

classics passes in shining brocade robes an
elder who holds and transmits the

original wisdom and he passes in the
middle of the bridge and looks

up at the moon
his face for that moment

splashed with distant silver
and he drops the book he was

holding with finger wedged in his place
that slips into the shining river

flowing below him and through our
rooms when we

wake up for a moment from our
deep sleep

the pages passing through us
and their words whispered etchedly

in our veins

2/21

## LIGHTNING BOLTS

Could lightning bolts be electric
rents in the sky-fabric

inadvertently revealing
the Next World's dazzle?

Heralded by thuds of
heavenly drawbridges?

Herds of sky cattle hooves
against arching bridge boards?

Light has to come through from there
and does so in flashes

Blinds us in this world to give us
insight into the next?

Hearts in our bodies
know these things already

lay down roads for God's
golden carts to cross

Our souls know so much more than
we do

More than even the
world knows

Thunder roll and lightning flash
bring all the worlds nearer

And the Lord of all the worlds
reflecting Himself to us

all that much
clearer

2/22

# THE PATH

You start early
you're nobody's fool

You set out on foot
no snow will stop you

Shapes in the mist
statues of warriors

Arms raised and weapons

You're undaunted
no footprints before you

You make your way

Wolf howls echo
Breath becomes audible

suddenly interior
You're walking inwardly

Sounds of footfalls
You're in the immaterial

A realm opens before you
traversed by saints before you

Now the way is clearer
though deep obscurity reigns

A landscape becomes sharper
deep colors appear

Rich greens and bright blues
echoes resounding around you

A path like glass or amber
cuts through the night like a flare

The black background of space dazzles
with its uncanny plethora of stars

Your heart's a steady beacon
your forehead's an unwavering beam

It's not where you're going that's wonderful
but the glory of where you are

No light can compare with this brilliance
nor description match its beauty

A magnificent wanderer's become you
breathless in a place of wonder

Who's coming toward you in silence?
Who are these walking with you?

It's not that their faces are obscured
their sheer radiance is blinding

A voice is actually calling you
A sound of clopping horse hooves

You're in a valley of light

Shapes of things are their meanings
speaking into the ears of your heart

suspended invisibly in space

in which knowledges are constantly pouring
inexpressible on human lips

understood in the land of this dwelling
before and after words are spoken

As the sky's planets shimmer their rainbows
and swirl their borealis glows

The dimensions open even farther
as if flowers bloomed backwards into being

Words are gone and
God's Presence mingles

What was thought is true
His embrace surrounds you

The impalpable becomes palpable
the conceived inconceivable

Crows fly in a blue sky
Yellow fields roll forward

What's before you is behind you
collapsing all around you

Who comes toward you is
for you alone

for your safe invitation
to leave it all behind you

each moment before you
from the tip of you to the soul of you

moving ever within you
each step ringing true

each gesture a worthy one
each silence a vocabulary

of unimpeachable significance
the air parting around you

The way forward abounding
nothing left of barriers

that really never existed
nothing left but to be

in the constant company
of companions of sublimity

as simple as a rooster
crowing the dawns awake

all life's light converging
just as it's dispersing

to its place of purest origin
in the golden curve of His Hands

suspended just as our hearts are
in this life-extinguishing air

our houses all dissolving
into their constituent atoms

our relationships all dissolving
into their innermost resonances

We're going ahead now without them
their cloaks whirl away completely

It's a sound of rushing water
over rocks made slippery by time

Who's there can't be named as alive
but never before as alive as now

This is what living was made for
this vivid incomparable sweetness

raining incessantly inside you
no further fire can extinguish it

imprinted as firmly on your heart
as when you were first conceived

This splendor more splendid than
silvery skies

stretched out on every horizon
this shapeless shape that awaits you

now that you've passed beyond
imprecation

to be called back to anything lesser
as indelible as your veins turned

inside-out in the next world
vividly present in this one

standing on the road you began on
even before you set out

morning birds in the silence
crickets quiet in daylight

Your sudden presence multiplied
into one beating heart in silence

not yours alone in time
but God's invisibly

whispering

2/24

## SONGS OF OUR SOULS

If we could string out the
songs of our souls

the way clotheslines are strung out
from building to building

or light years are strung out from
star to star

including seismic rumbles and
something opening its eyes for the

first time

If they could burst like gunshots
and absorb all gunshots

and these songs had within their tones
canyonic and abysmal silences

that dissolve matter the way icebergs
are weeping into the seas

their streaks of otherworldly blue turning
gray in the cold sunlight

but our soul-songs with projectile direction
honing past molecular obstruction

themselves rising from realms free of
molecular obstruction

to flow to where ears who
hear them are rubbed into the

forward thrust of their streams

with no turning from right to left
or from left to right

but straight shots to the heart

collecting as the songs go
other souls within their sails

along the undersides of clouds
and textures of fur on creaturely backs

who raise their heads at midnight
to cry to the moon

the songs of our souls
part of that cry

and its melodiously reflective response

from tree to tree and stone to stone
throughout the worlds

that we might stand with the

songs of our souls shining from our

faces from face to face of us one at a
time and all at once

in this godly earth God's given us
earth to earth and galaxy to

galaxy one sung note in our
breaths from our souls enough

to ignite in all of us His Light
throughout

2/25

## THE JOYS OF A BREATH

The joys of a breath filled with
remembrance of God

is field after field of golden pastureland
the grasses all bending one direction

straightening up in the crisp air

The mysterious interlocking years of that air
keeping rust off the machinery of space

by turning like plants on their pivots

or the flight of a few thousand parrots
through dark red canyons in shadow

bursting into a blue sunlight

or everyone on earth at the same time
going about their business

and suddenly feeling joy
leaving off even murder for a moment

to flick off joy from their lips and eyelids

for its flood flashes through village and
metropolis taking posh restaurant and

poor fishing shanty in its wake

remembrance from tree to tree connecting the
living dots across earth and leaving not a

dot behind
from under the *ba* of *bismillah*

in the Name of Allah

*ameen*

                                                                                     3/1

# THE PUZZLE

Put the puzzle on its end
and shake the pieces out

One continent fits so snugly
against another

Look around but see with
double sight

What passes for cars and trees
are trees and cars passing or

things that pass
as we pass

Somehow it's always to do with
sweet

obliteration

Leaving one thing
going to the next

while it's the same thing in unutterably
gorgeous transformation

coming round again to meet us
from behind or

in front

Flamey tiger eyes suddenly become
exotic

flashing all around us

or blank looks from the same seagulls
time after time

circling overhead
as we circle below them

*"Come over here"* says the ocean
*"and listen to my sighs —*

*sun moon rain or shine
I never miss a beat"*

*"Come up here"* say clouds
always in a hurry to scurry along

*"and see yourself from our vapid
perspective"*

But slow or fast
they're rapidly gone

taking their "perspective"
with them

*"Come over here"* say graves
*"or can't you stand their*

*depth? Just because*
*grass grows over us doesn't mean we're*

*not part of the puzzle"*

Don't pull your sad face around
snowmen

come spring
just because they can't

hold their own

A river runs through us
from every direction

that we should
launch ourselves out on

before opportunity
passes us by

completely

3/21

# PERSPICACIOUS

*"Perspicacious"* has nothing to do with
perspiring

and *"seditious"* may have nothing or
everything to do with *"thirst"* as the word

*"sed"* in Spanish means *"thirst"*

and *"tendency"* has no relationship to
ten people living in a residence

and so on and on in the lovely way we say
everything and imagine words are actually related to

the things they relate (linguists please forgive me)
but there's a shimmer in language that

radiates its own calm glow even as the
world it refers to may seem to be a

crystalline palace on a quartz hill in sunlight
wordlessly halo'd in its own cat-like

silence except for occasional
yowls and growls

by day or night

Our good Lord Adam stood unperplexed by God's
*fiat* of his sudden linguistic flow

and each objective thing took on a new
light in shudders of languages like

taffeta flaps or gauze wing wrappings from
Sumerian to modern Japanese for the exact

same things sitting in their own world
exactly the same but by different names

Naming names us in our essential
unnamable essences

but meanwhile our tongues like
waterfalls cascade through words as

fast as thought can bounce them off the
greatest and most flexible muscle in our

bodies

giving voice to our immense and perspicacious
awe as well as our impossible and glorious

dreams

3/22

## A SUNSET

The delicious plump koi-fish
color of the sky
shimmering veils
across more bombastic ignitions

of fiery gas-ball galaxies engorged and
exploding arrays of tails whose vast
heads invisible in expanses of ether
babble crescendos in God's Hearing

having been so animated by His
Speaking in spatially
comprehensible sentences that say

*"All is nothing before Incandescence
the igneous Sovereignty
one godly flame-tip enough
to illuminate all earths and heavens*

*that burst in
sunset's eyesight
then death's heart's delight that's
cloaked by a starry night's dark knell*

*shut tight"*

3/22

PROSTRATION

To do the prostration in prayer
like stroking the soft warm

fur of a cat

and its purr

3/24

# IN SWITZERLAND

## 1

Let's see

I'm heading toward death at the
same speed this airplane is

heading toward Switzerland

Alps out the window are clouds
or the clouds are Alps

but in mistier formation

Spread-out cities of night
or are those the stars?

Endless dimensions
or are those my breaths?

If you hold your handspan in front of you
that's your entire existence

God's blip
equals your Eternity

Incarnate every corner of it
completely

Not a whisker less

If we turn away from it for a moment
a little door squeezes shut in a

tiny wall meant for us alone

Somewhere on a table
a crystal beams light in all directions

and the light in our faces is
some of that light

and the shimmer from the highest
waterfall in the world is

some of that light

and as He bends over the bright world
God's Compassion is

all of that light

Not a corner left unlit

heading toward Switzerland

as fast as our death is

Not a whisker less

## 2

I got up from the dead and walked

Weeds and webs dissolved from
around me

The hand that touched me back to life
was light

A small corridor became a wheatfield
in sunlight

A small door became the open sky

Loved ones flew in flocks and
landed on branches

Their songs were variegations of a sweet theme

Sparkles dazzled their melodies

To walk this way took inhuman effort
since what pushed me forward was

God
beyond theology

To get up from the dead
having died so slowly

one of God's mysteries
and a prophetic prerogative

to irradiate His splendor

Since the soul takes on its colors
flesh is just one of them

We go from life to life at ease

You can see it in animals
who have no self consciousness

they romp and sleep
stand in elegance

and go on to something else
forever

After a few steps
I leant on a doorjamb

looking out

Mountains and rivers
extend into the far distance

I will or will not go there

but there they are

## 3

The wind sounds everywhere the same
whenever it blows

The heart of the believer knows what it knows
wherever it goes

A forest of trees obstructs the view of a
sunlit sky

In the dark the universe opens itself
to the believing eye

Silence falls and brings its clouds of
radiant rain

Each second brings its godly gifts of
loss and gain

Alive or dead the soul moves on to the
Promised Land

Wind and trees and dark and silence
and grains of sand


## 4

An elephant forgot itself for a moment and
wanted to fly

so it closed its eyes

What borders and boundaries do we have
that in themselves haven't got

perfectly serviceable wings?

Nothing too high or too low seems to
stop us

Knowing that if we swing too high for the
natural tensions of gravity we could

fly free or fail in a downward Icaristic trajectory

or if we aim too low or not low enough
could remain on the surface in an

artful but immobile design
inert forever

Not so the elephant
soaring over Switzerland

the Alps like ants below it as it
swayed slowly back and forth above their frosted toothy

peaks

Entering a divine domain has its
particular dangers and challenges

altitude only one of them
and holding to horizontality against

prevailing winds another
if God grants us the pachydermial luck

to transcend our mortal dimensions
and the weight of our improbable tusks

5

The swamp boat blew its whistle as it
rounded the bend in the

Noknoko River and the
swamp snakes hung down from the

Blooban trees

*Noknoko River in Switzerland?*

My usual angels must be
napping (but angels don't sleep)

And I imagine thousands of them
picnicking on Wordsworth's daffodils

(but angels don't eat) their wide
wings softly folding over the bending

yellow daffodil heads under a
blinding blue morning sky

And the captain of the swamp boat
knocks his meerschaum against the

bow and startles a
flock of flamingos who suddenly

pink the sky with their flight
like busy flames

And the secret cargo which is
no longer secret in this

telling of it is sticks of celestial
dynamite to ignite us into

consciousness that simultaneously
renders all our experiential world thoroughly

transparent in a flash more blinding even than
that blue sky but just as

crowded if not more compactly
crowded with angels

as I write this by flashlight
in our bedroom in Switzerland

seeing through the walls

to where you are

---

(Note: This poem written in the dark of our bedroom while visiting our son and his family in Buchrain near Zurich, Switzerland. I made up the Amazonian sounding names for river and trees, *Noknoko* River and *Blooban Trees*, pausing before the first a bit before taking a stab at it. Later that day we went to Lucerne, and walking through the narrow shop streets my son pointed out the children's clothing store he said was where his wife spends all their money. The name of the store, unusual in Switzerland: *Noknok*. I swear! Amazed, I asked his Swiss wife what this strange name might mean in Swiss German... she had no clue, and admitted its strangeness...)

# 6

O God of the false start and the
perfect landing

of the compass point and the
point of no return

of notes in the margin and the
margin of error

of mahogany forests and a
thicket of lies

God of all we can enumerate
be with us now

Of stallions and stagnation of lions and their
roars of the silence of giraffes and the

looks of lemurs
of nothing we can see and all that we

survey

God of all this and all that
be with us now

God of pride and its deflation
of anger and its pacification

of rowing to safety and losing
courage

of the sharp shooter and the last gasp
of the shadow of the tower and its

staunch resistance
in all kinds of weather battered and

bruised
be with us now

Thimbles and brain pans eye sockets and
islands

everything we can imagine and
everything we can't

O God until we're driven past
insanity to where nothing of this world

matters in the least
yet everything worthy of your love

is worthy of our love
and loved in return

beyond what we know of it
in the entire ocean of its force over us

down to the last hair
split and the last objection diminished

God of all this
be with us now

and forever


7

The alienation of existentialism turns out to be:
*Psychological*


8

I'd like to hew as fine a line in the
line of a poem as the

hairline crack in a piece of fine porcelain
or a fault line through a stand of oaks

or the lines on the face of a Mongolian sheepherder
having weathered eighty winters and still's

wrinkled with radiant laughter

As fine a line as from here by laser to
Jupiter or farther

As fine a line as the DNA of prophets and
saints gene by generous gene

finer than the linkage of our years on earth
as fine as the evolution from reptiles to birds

God having willed wings to lizards to let them
take to the skies and

fly away

To somehow hew so closely to the
finest sense of spirit and the

fiery spark of spirit-sensation
yet somehow beyond the spiritual

of the way deer see things or swooping owls
or the electric shiver that rises through everything on its

way from God back to
God again

## 9

The blind in the dark see light
from the dark side

A tunnel through a mountain leads to a
different weather

The heart in its travels advances with a
backpack of intentions

Will this poem crack open to reveal an
igneous center?

Will the Switzerland around us revolve into a
feathery plain

and each zipper of its quills call out
one of God's Names?

It's 3 A.M. and these hard-won lines are
growling

Feeding time in the day
satisfaction in the

heart of night?

But I can't sleep when the white wind
blows all around me

Nothing is left where it was and nothing has
quite found its new

resting place

Is this the river that isn't the same even the
first time we step into it?

Are the planets moving so fast we'll
never keep up with them?

Has the heart ever seen such wonders?
Can we even begin to count them before

their silvery curtain falls again to reveal
another miracle horde?

Things reaching out from within themselves
to be so sweetly acknowledged?

The wind whirls around on the mountains
causing soft snow to stir

Everywhere the windows of our faces go up
to reveal our true faces beneath

One bridge worth crossing can be
crossed far more than once

Each circumstance has its locked doors
and its open road

Each interim is a universe waiting to be
explored

No one is exempt from stepping forward
when the time comes

In the sounds of Light angels can be
heard breathing

That icy high-pitched sound in our ears
is their swirling flight

Come closer my dear ones so you can
inspect my innermost heart

There's no fear at the station of expectation
but that shows the way for everything to come

The shattering roar of the lion at the end of the road
is only the beginning

The tag ends of our lives are
drawn in so neatly at the end

And at our beginnings we start again


10

I find it incredibly strange to be
flying home from

Switzerland to Philadelphia
in midair in a metal lozenge with wings

full of people sleeping or watching a
movie or reading when we should all be

down on our knees as in a Medieval icon
neat row after neat row of us

praying to God *(isn't God
nearer up here?)* with all His rather stiff

horizontal angels like floating gossamer banners
around our trajectory forward

for seven or eight hours straight!

Like a great whale lumbering through the
sky full of Geppettos and Pinocchios

scheming how to get
out into the open again and on

solid ground or at least continue
floating upward to Paradise's domain

all gold leaf and icy trumpets

But we lumber on grinding our motors
jittery through turbulence

eating pretzels or
going to the bathroom!

*Going to the bathroom?*

*Miles above the earth?*

3/26-4/3

## ALONG THE WAY

Along the way watch out for
antlered toads and

the occasional banshee
giraffes as tall as you that

look you straight in the eye

an owl as it swivels its
head in your direction and its

steady stare
strikes like lightning

The sheer cliff of polished opals
that gleam all the way down its

fall into a delicious chasm

When the earth's pulled out from
under us we can't always

fly

The motor below us
grinds to its destination

As earth dwellers we can only
hope for the best

As sky dwellers we're
already there

wearing its furry hats
sailing its boats

This poem born of a pain in my
lower back from

falling flat on it yesterday

Everyone was very kind
saying *"Stay still"*

*"Would you like a drink of water?"*
*"Get up slowly"*

One door closes
another opens

I swear to you
God's in the details

Moss can't grow on a
whirling tree

The heart remains with its
eyes fixed to its eyepiece

though shaken like a leaf

# THEY LET ME DOWN SLOWLY

They let me down slowly
It could have happened a lot faster

They let me down slowly
and then gave me a smart whack on my

back from the floor

But they held my shoulders and slowly
let me fall backwards the angels who

grace every fall with their own slow motion
from every height

Napoleon toppling from his horse
a child down stair after stair

They're with us all the time
easing us into even the worst situations

I could feel them letting me fall
slowly to the slick floor where I slid

and looking back up at them
into the concerned faces looking down

## THE WATERS OF NIGHT

The waters of night surround us
with their spooky coos

and sawing through the
length and breadth of them are

bioluminous populations of souls
endlessly circulating

and down at the very bottom where
no light goes

are the most wonderful ceremonies
robed figures moving in slo-mo procession

as watery as the water is
but of such noble bearing

nobody dare gainsay them
wrapped in floating weeds of

flickering incandescence and each
carrying a flag with our

faces on them beaming through the
filmy brine in deepest

inky darkness where

no light goes

more pitch black than any blackness
known

more like the spaces between stars

each face of ours in
miles down luminosity

eyes more shining than Saturn
each forehead a continent of

singing birds
hearing through the waters

this comprehensible song
linking us soul by soul

in deepest down darkness
each heart of ours thumping

with the soul's heartbeat

the soul's home

4/9

## SILVER LADDER

A silver ladder burnished of human breaths
should be enough to

climb to the heights

The air smelling of cinnamon
rainbow wheels turning across the

horizon where a giant's gaze has
grazed the grasslands

and the sky rolls back its heavy wooden doors
to let the stars in

each one countable and accountable for the
treasures of its lights spread across

an emptiness wider than the fullest known
entity in existence

whose waves we blow across to calm
and whose peace falls softly on us

when we glow

4/10

# THE WEIGHT OF THE WORLD

The weight of the world was
suddenly lifted from him

and everything solid became
structures of transparent silvery butterflies

which for a car or train on its
track over there might be

sweet as they disperse into thin air

The Grand Canyon itself was
another matter altogether

And he himself at once buoyant both
internally and externally

so that the most ancient tune to
humankind began harmonicaing his

lips from depths he'd never
noticed before

and when he himself found himself
similarly dispersing

it was a bright tangible
melody in all directions at once

and nothing left anywhere in the entire world
but a kind of

metrical fluttering

4/12

## HORSES OF FAJR

I wake to find
the horses are ready

for fajr prayer
sleek and shining

silvery as water
dark and fair

Blacks and sorrels
browns and whites

a herd of light
wild horses

freshly emerged from the
wilds of night

manes of lightning
hooves of thunder

the elements tamed
the distant horizon

veiled in snow
and flickering flame

4/13

# THE DAY COMES

The day comes
when every boulder will be
rolled into place
every tree will have reached its
apogee
every river will achieve the
symphony all that sweet and
terrible rushing of water has aimed for

and the sky like a distant backdrop all those
millennia will enter our
lives in the most intimate way
where starlight from our
eyes and extremities is the
norm

Measurements will have
disappeared and in their place
a curious rippling of everything into its
interlocked connection with
everything else in matter and space

*Has that day already come?*

It has
for some

4/14

## SINGLE POINTED

What we say to others resounds down
glittery tubing into our hearts

There's a wall of world that goes up behind
everything made of

thin transparent sheets
slimmer than breath

that extends all the way into the
next world

If we strike a match in front of it
its flame is mirrored a

thousand times into the void

Strange wingéd fish might float across it

Sandstorms of diamonds might blow across it

We'll cross it on foot and go to the
other side to see ourselves where we

are now exactly where we
were before crossing

but transformed into blue wind

giant grasshoppers
bigger than light

hopping away in all directions
making their high-pitched nostalgic music

a song drifting over the whole scene
we can't quite place

but that we know in our bones

a slanted light lighting up a
corner never before seen

confined by nowhere we can see
since it's

nowhere to be seen

The self's peacock
shrieking its relief and

landing in a tree

God's Light pouring down the stairs

Night crossing its own path
with a path of silver

one step at a time
that lifts our feet and

turns our
heads in eternity's direction

as single-pointed
as a star

4/16

# TOUCHSTONE

The touchstone here
is any who hears the
Name of Allah
turns to gold
or in the case of the heart
a river

A sapling becomes a
tree in an instant
the eye
a seer centuries old
or in the case of the greedy
a giver

He suffices for all that
we have or do
light or dark
heat or cold
and all that's not truly us
we sever

Call it Truth or
simply Belief
something we've
bought that was sold
that rather than be a
stone we're
a believer

But our days have been
burnished to a greater shine
opening after opening
fold after fold
And of what we could not
do before
we deliver

                                            4/17

## SOMEBODY'S KNOCKING

> *A la porte de la maison qui viendra frapper?*
> *Une porte ouverte on entre*
> *Une porte fermée un antre*
> *Le monde bat de l'autre coté de ma porte*
> — Pierre Alber Birot

Somebody's knocking at the
door to be let in

Sounds like a woodpecker from
across a dark and lonely forest

We have to go deeper now to
find the thread

lost at birth

though it hooked us up instantly
to this land of incessant knocking

and brought us face to face
with the door that

must be knocked on to be let in
the knocking upon which

assures we'll be let in

or maybe not for some souls
who haven't found the rhythm

or have let the first silence
from the other side

discourage them
from within

                                                  4/20

# EQUIPOISE

The causation of equipoise
back far enough to where the

first spark plugged in

The eye blink of desert ibis
or swoop of sparrow flock

back far enough to
slant of planet times

flap of wings equals
push of surf in far Madagascar

or the rippling folds in pink and
purplish stripes in the

Northern Lights over Kamchatka

If we go back and back
(or even forward and forward

in the cone of time that reverses
so that where we are now is also

back and back)
in a space as vast as a gnat's eyebrow

at the flick of a song swelling the
throat of a girl waiting with her

poison dart for a
rainbow-colored parrot to fly by

or from side to side
where the trade winds suddenly take a

tack to the right as the
great baritone molten blob of the sun sets

into the sea's inscrutable blackness

Or the delicate sound of a high sung note in the
air as it trembles next to distant

hyena's laughter and
takes on a certain shimmer as the girl

lifts her bamboo pipe to her
lips to send the poison dart flying

its prototype predecessors back and
back in time like flipping

film frames in perfect time-lapse
to the first dart perfected and

propelled to its suddenly vulnerable
feathery destination

who back far enough was a fledgling
just leaving its nest

in the circular scheme of things
whose globular rotations continue

at the gong sound of the
causation of everything's equipoise

where we hear the
reverberations of every

permutation from then on
henceforward

and the divine pulse whispering along each
stem and wind pipe

each shiver of elephants pouring across a
green veldt at sunrise

each seeing eye sweeping
expanse in beauty's original display

shuddering sky down simplicity
of God's complicity

light upon light
from first beam brightness

to dark upon dark
from first dog's bark

4/29

## SOMETHING

Something in the air
or in the earth
reminds us of our life
or of our death

a golden knob that
glimmers in the light
or something low
that slithers through the night

a flake of something
passing in our space
a few scant inches
right before our face

reflects back to our
invisibility
the vanity of our
invincibility

falling into the
dark heart of ourselves
to see what jewels might
light our inner shelves

and God Who lights the
longest corridor
is He Who answers
the knocks on every door

though nothing might be
there that we can see
yet all is nothing
but ungendered He

and without Him
no existency
embodies our
invisibility

4/30

## TO REACH THE WATER

To reach the water
we ride the waves

To reach the roof
we ride the sky

To reach to where we're not
we achieve

the elegant intention God's
intended for us

going where none's been before
our gentle entrance

where we've seen its circling
circumstances

beckoning their oceanic fronds
in invitation to arrive

at an unforeseen but
destined destination

Turn this around
we're already there

So why haven't mountains
opened their crystal corridors

leading to God's
unseen splendors?

Or is it our cloud-eyes
can't focus on their

hidden scintillations
all along

all around us
all the time?

4/30

# LAST DAY

If the last day were here
I wonder whose chimes would ring

whose spotted horses would override their
corrals

how whale pods might react
and the noise they'd make in their

piccolo oboe songs and
interlocking circles

swimming tighter and tighter to a
spiraling center to finally

disappear

And if the fiery gates of the mountains would
fling open and shepherds

lead their sheep to safety as promised

and how high waves would have to reach
before cresting in curls around

all the continents

and who from the centers of the great
cities both past and present

would run into public spaces
confessing their sins and the

sins of their nations

and if roadways' asphalts would melt and
run in rivers to the boiling seas

and if we sang out our songs to the
heavenly regions their legions might

relent and by relenting lead to
our final and grateful release

though nothing but ultimate
ash be left floating in the

silvery nothing of the air

finally leading by Divine Grace to
nowhere

but
just *there*

5/1

# VANISHING HORIZON

Underwater and underground
run deep streams of memory

Those who latch onto them
hear a river of voices great as

the sky

Dead voices persistent in their
proclamations their piteous laments

wishing their memories had funneled
in one direction and one direction only

Enormous cascade of the glorious
Creator's silent chromatic

melodious bellows magnificent and
invisibly fiery igniting everything with

being into being
from toad's footprint to exploding

sunset on a hill
to saliva in our throats

water that slakes our thirst
and drops of light that assuage

our heart's dark grief

Is there anyone here
who doesn't hear this river

these streaming clear enunciations
that link us in all directions

to those who've gone before
even one nanosecond before this one

and how they stand in us full height
straining to see past

the already vanishing
horizon?

5/5

# NAKED BEFORE MY CAT

Standing naked in front of my cat
should I show some modesty?

She doesn't seem to care
I'm not covered in fur

yet I feel a shy kinship
that connects us in a forest air

of delicate indications and averted or
steady gaze

all planetary mammals whoever we are
of whatever size

eyes and hearts a single seer
however many legs we have

whether or not we're shy or brash
coming out of our cave into

full daylight
naked in the air

## WHERE THE GREATEST WISDOM IS

Where the greatest wisdom is
is a pewter dish in a

room filled with light

at the base of a chasm of basalt
and the sun tilted on top

like a purple feather in flames

How do you get there
except on your own speed

and with silence at your lips
and boundaries falling away

in your heart

who has had the rigorous
training of stallions

and the motherly compassion
of mares

whose tongues lick off the
afterbirth to let the

light out?

How do we get there
except by the bricked up door of

God's Grace when
He decides to make its bricks

traces

and the road traveled to be the
very place of its manifestation

His touch all over you

His taste in your mouth?

5/11

## LOTUS IN REVERSE

If it's a matter of sinking into the
earth at last

the way a hippo sinks into mud
or angels sink through

clouds of light

or in reverse illumination a
lotus sinks up through the

surface of a pond in an
inverted vision to

open its golden petals to the
sun that we can see

but the dead sink down
to where we can

no longer see
into a world beyond

visibility

What do we
take to that land

and what do we leave behind

that would strike someone blind
with light?

Our own light
sublime?

The earth rises above us
as we descend

all its people
antlike now

continuing their
restless striving above ground

as we like angels
sink through

clouds of light
to what's now deemed as

dark
but unseen

as our hearts like the lotus
break up through

the surface of night

5/16

## WE COULD DRY UP

We could dry up
like the leaf I found

plastered flat inside my
slipper thinking it was the

nap inside worn smooth

or else kept plump and
ripe by God's Light?

In any case leaf-lacy
body in flakes

spirit kept green and
free

5/16

## IF I TURNED INTO DEATH

If I turned into death
would death turn into an acorn

and would the acorn fall onto a
glass rod and would the

glass rod break into bits?

All this in front of a green sunset?

There's no telling where this could go
though the gate is wide open and

all the white horses are
fleeing up the hill into a single silver flame

Go now and scale the tree to its top
and collect the colored

lights you find there

If the black cloth fell across the
window we couldn't make out all the

radiant faces coming toward us

But dense matter intervenes and
dark matter dispels the darkness

so unless you sing the entire song
each word fitted into place

each note burnished to a sheen

then death sits hard on a soft place
and soft on a hard place

and never tips its hand
until the song is done

                                                                    5/17

# AT THE SQUARE EDGE

> *"Success in circuit lies"*
> — Emily Dickinson

At the square edge of this
round earth in the

triangular circle
whose clouds elongate into

words and stretch into
sentences

long enough for whole populations of
migrating birds to rest on

on their way to the sun
whose squarish circularity

spitfire and rotational
can be depended on for a few more

millennia God willing
at the hot center of our galaxy

and the epicenter of our
undivided attention

for the fractional century of our
lifetime while we

go about our business of
living scattering clutter and

sweeping it into a pan then just as
quickly scattering more

that even filters in
dust particles through the atmosphere

that we in physiological gratitude
breathe

in thought trains and little
air puffs enough to keep us

going and coming through these
seasonal tunnels of

light and shade
at the square edge of this

round earth in the
triangular circle

whose clouds elongate into
words and stretch into

sentences

where we find ourselves
pondering God's most

elegant geometries
that just continue

adding and subtracting us
and everything within and

around us vanishing quite
cunningly into His

thin air wherein true darkness
dazzles brighter than any possible

ray or dot of light

5/20

## I FLOAT IN A SEA

I float in a sea of
God-light and poetry

but you might not know it
to see me

bending to greet a spider
skittering across a sill

letting a fly out
when the

night is still

What blanket of obscurity
covers us all

where Allah has

placed us
on this revolving ball

to climb His darkness and
swim His Light

with hearts much softer
than anthracite?

5/21

# I GET READY FOR SLEEP

I get ready for sleep

I roll the cart into the barn and
tuck birds' heads under their wings

soak up puddles from the road
and turn trees to the east

Rabbits are already curled up in their
dens all white circles of fur

as silent in their snoozing as the
night itself

I put my eyeglasses on a shelf with no
eyes behind them

where they take on a ghostly cast
and pull four walls around me

to narrow my compass

If antlers go by
I'm unafraid

The taller the stag the greater the
ceremony that might

lead in the light between its
jagged horns to a glimpse or vision

before my sleep is ended
under the skull roof's

glassy gate
*O my God!*

5/27

# A LONG SESSION OF NON SEQUITURS

It's a long session of non sequiturs
that we're here then we're gone

we're up we're down
a boat is in the sea then the

sea is in the boat

conundrums litter
paradox path

Gone today here tomorrow
like in a mosaic haphazardly

placed front ones in back
back ones in front

I'm my own father's son
and I'm my own son's father

back and back backtracking
standing in place

all things changed utterly
and nothing changed

each moment standing out
from all the rest

all gone in a wink
before you can think

or try to calculate
what's what

Cow on a roof
stomping her hoof

Rainbow in space
Astonishment's face

                                                                 5/28

## WATER THAT TRICKLES

The water that trickles through our blood
is the first water from before the Flood

and on that water floats a golden boat
that we're inside of from toes to throat

"Incubus" you say? — no — *not at all*
The secret of our secret from before the Fall

Slosh and globular wish-wash and clear
The path of each heartbeat brings us near

That first beat perpendicular to the godly Throne
taking us nearer to His blessed Zone

Floodwater fascination magnetized beat
puts us squarely on the Mercy Seat

5/31

## PARADISE OF BUZZES

Our Lord —
who stumble down a rockface

to open our ocean hearts
rock by rock

Lord out of this abyss
that is in fact our bliss

turned inside-out
all natural as a beehive

sprung out of nowhere
hanging from eaves

in a Paradise of buzzes

How quick the
bubble bursts that

shuts us in

or the ocean's horizon in us
extended out farther

than under the sun

6/1

## WHAT IS LOST

A huge blue wind blows
or at the moment a huge blue wind

doesn't seem to blow but all seems
perfectly serene

and erases itself and its antecedents
entirely away as if

no door ever opened and then
quietly shut

no eyes ever flickered in a snowstorm
or any mouth having all its

teeth and a perfect tongue and glottis
ever spoke and after such

eloquence was silent again

It's a huge blue folder of wind
that keeps everything

in order category by category

It's a rhinoceros of air
or better yet a vapor hippo

with that maw of a mouth and those
ivory pegs for teeth

yawning wider than life itself
to snap shut on it all as if it

never was

Perhaps God means it this way for us
to better focus on His Majestic

acts rather than their hypnotic
productions

even to the total disappearance of
former worlds with all their

dinosaurs and memories like bear traps
around both our ankles at once

Try serenity from the start
emptiness as normal protocol

Light lighting up a space that's already
well enough lit

or dark so dark pitch blackness
has to put itself alongside it

to judge just how really dark it is
to start with

where even the richest darkness is
light enough after all

and both light and dark a
perfect frame for the

blue wind vacuum heartbeat
chamber of total apprehension of

God's awesome
wonderfulness in the What-He-Is of it

without precedent nor antecedent
in the total and everlasting

shut-upness of it all
never again and forevermore

lost in pure bliss
in a bright blue as blue as

bright blue ever was and then
even bluer than that

*amen*

6/2

## SINCE WHEN DID THE WORLD

Since when did the world we
wake into look so peaceful?

The walls lined with books the
furniture staying in place

the piles neat and dust mostly invisible

a tranquility of things

and when I opened my eyes at
first I saw red kaleidoscope patterns

and heard only the whirr of the
standing fan

and a sense of extended space out there
beyond what my eyes see

but in dream it can all be tumbling
or wildly transforming

The ship moving at odd angles
to the rest of it all

and the rest of it all
in mist

6/3

## THE CERTAIN GAZE THE SKY HAS

The certain gaze the sky has
looking at us in the rain

drenching our clothes
wanting to embrace us but

keeping its distance
not in an anthropomorphic way

All this and the world's animation
like tall grasses

ticking their time
blade by blade as erect as

passing Roman soldiers
from the heroic age

slippering by blade by blade
somehow shouldering their swords

(which they would never do
an awkward image that

imposed itself
when I try so hard here

to let things do as they do

in "reality"

except when clouds
let down their gangplanks

and lit with light or
darker than the darkest dark

angels flow into our space
and circulate the big and

small dimensions
each presenting a face of

uttermost comeliness
like a perfect baby's lunar roundness

and piercing gentle eyes
of hot blue light

and round soft cheeks
of uttermost softness

in full flight
around us)

6/8

# TIME GOES SO FAST

Time goes so fast
and my life grows so short!

I look at my watch
and look again

*it's an hour later!*

Even my imagined horses grow
gray beards in the wind

and trees outside get
sooty leaves

*"So much to do"* I say to myself
but gone before I know it!

Who's left to stay the course?
Who left to go past sharp corners

into open space?

Sitting here writing it down
tightens time's skein

But when I look at my watch again
and the choir has grown silent

out the black window
it's an hour later already

*or two or three!*

There's a train of thin air that
comes all around us and

moves us down the track
but there's also the famous

unwobbling pivot that moves but
doesn't wobble in the

heart

If we sit in the vestibule outside
God's Good-Pleasure Place forever

won't that bring time to a full
stop?

From our place
to His "place"

moving
immovably

along?

6/13

## ITS SILVER THREADS

He left even his body behind
when he set out through glassy forests and

down rivers in bamboo boats lashed
together with thongs

and drifted forward on water currents and
air currents to the simple heartbeat

rhythms that similarly compel all things
forward

endlessly forward
all our faces facing there with high

hopes and expectations

and the years he spent with shepherds and
astronomers professors of round earth and

flat cloud striders and amorphous
altitudinous climbers

saints in their grass huts and
golden nimbuses

fragments of time compounded into
breathable bits

all enabled him at the end to
smile holding onto the Prophet's hem

being helped into heaven by the
intricate stitches of its

scintillant and sacred sewing
its eloquent and endless

silver threads

6/17

# THE SAVAGE IN THE LAMPLIGHT

The savage in the lamplight
casts his spell on the

roadside roses

and out of the funny darkness
neon flashes become things of

daylight's uses

Geometrical spectacle we move in
leaning against this or that we think

will support us
when all this complex just as

easily collapses and
goes back into its darkness

like into stables their
obedient horses

Even our galaxy like a
twinkling thing from afar

seen in its grandeur and glory
a twinkle among trillions of stars

blinking like indeterminate
silver

a flutter among this universe's
flurry a generous giver

on its way to contemplate and be
contemplated by His intrinsic

journey of simply Himself
a single and singularly multiple river

watching us through His own eyes
unlike all others

yet also as alike as those of our
fathers and mothers

6/18

## WAKING UP IN THE SAME ROOM

Waking up in the same room you
fell asleep in

*what a miracle!*
So much has moved since falling into

so deep a sleep

Tectonic plates have shifted under
foot and finny

waters washed whole continents
ashore

Births and deaths
a miracle our eyes don't catch

Casablanca Corsica Madagascar
Siam

pink flotillas and sampans on
black canals as serene as moonlight

or flat into blood revolutions in
backwaters blasts and past caring

but to open eyes and flick on the light
in the same room they shut on

all geometrically in the same place

roof overhead floor below
no wild foxes surrounding the bed

no whales wide-jawed awesomely
surrounding our bodies with their dark

or maybe things have changed utterly
and we with them

*Captain Bligh Captain Ahab Captain my*
*Captain our fearful trip is done*

crashed and beached
forevermore alone

                                                        6/19

# IS THAT HIS LOVE?

Allah covers us
like the softest inside of a

leather glove all around us

Is that our skin
*or is that His love?*

He wants grass under our feet
and sky above us

He comes all round us and
all the way through us

Is that the world
*or is that His love?*

If we stand in the rain
His wetness will soak us

and keep us dry

In an avalanche
what keeps us falling is His

falling with us
before us and after us

The air He gives us to breathe
is the air that kills us

Is that the Angel of Death facing us
*or is that His love?*

I see the plains He calls us to
have never been seen by anyone

except through His love for us

The ache and pain and
hammering

fiery camels and
slowdowns and blights

His river of sound that always
engulfs us

Stops and starts that
seem like movement

Stillness that
never leaves us

Is that His distance
very far from us

*or is that His love?*

The beating at the heart of us
companion through all of this

*is that His love?*

The bridge He gives us
to cross over to

what is true of us

glass or cement or
stopped breath or sighs

These very eyes that see
glisten and scintillation

that never stop their
incessant pouring around us

and the softness like the
inside of a

leather glove all around us

inside and out and
inside-out all of us

Is that His intimacy
neverendingly

touching us
*Is that His love?*

6/21

# THEY SAY

## 1

They say the door is too
small to fit through

but the garden on the other side
so luminous and new

glows like a heartbeat inside us
and what do we care about

door frames?

We want a path where
each rock sings

and people are mute

Each tree shakes with that
particular shaking

that chimes with our own
down to our marimba bones

in air made audible
by the colors around us

each yellow yawn

a gong

each blue murmur
a rivering mirror

and no step taken
that doesn't lead us farther

to what was never far
and couldn't be nearer

Each red glimmer
sharper than silver

His Face of Beauty
that makes us believers

His Face of Majesty
that makes Eternity shiver

and echo there
forever in our

livers


2

That's where a gazelle spoke first
and a giraffe bent down to

listen

Deer antlers gleamed in the dark
and furry paws caressed the

black grass under us

*"It couldn't be clearer"*
and then silence surrounded it

and it hung in the air

*"A Face so pure"*
as water nearby carried its

glimmer everywhere

*"Turning and turning to our
pool's interior"*

all those beast eyes
charged with His Grandeur

more than our poor eyes
can garner

our silent partners

Then the rose spoke
and broke the silence

and nothing was what it was
nor the same as before

we went through that door


3

At the level of the air
we could see as far

as behind us coming near

and past what we took to be us
in all our hopes and fears

more like broken than brokers
more like sounded than sounders

in the resonant air
a string touched

that makes everything clear

shivering there
as everywhere

6/25

## GET UP OUT OF SOUND SLEEP

Get up
out of sound sleep

like someone
poking up from the ground

or through one of the heavens
poked entirely through

to the other side
face reflecting the stars

as far as you can see
until your place of origin

becomes you
poking through

You've seen the
blood river flowing below you

the animal stampede to
brighter air

their faces averted
hearts full of care

Wear their shirts on your back

but beware

The heart has its Path
where no teeth gnash

nor eyes burn
and the sun doesn't rise

from the east
but glows in our center

with benevolent face
in interior space

6/27

## ANSWER ENOUGH

The attempt to speak commands a
gathering of squirrels

when keeping silent is an
apter reply

to the avalanche of stimulus
before us

with its visual puns and aural
acrobatics that keep our

tympanum's bongos busy

One word and it's all over
the last barrel with soft human center

over the Niagara

The sudden stillness on a
subway train deep underground already

and no one dead

Let us speak as deer talk
in high-pitched alertness

listening as far as possible

to the outer reaches of our forest

for crack of hoof or scratch of paw in the
twiggy underbrush

and a silken rainbow be our tongue
its colors shimmering

the sound of the river itself to itself
Allah to Allah

answer enough
murmuring

    6/30

## GOD'S ONE DAY

In every dreaded corner
danger lies

In every beauteous
road's curve

beauty's eyes catch
beauty by surprise

The tiger's maze-striped
symmetrical back

arched over the dark

In dark's depths the
shadow green eye-gleam

of the lonely shark

Shrink all light to a dot
dazzling in our brows

above our eyes

in every space we inhabit
whatever shape or size

as it elaborately unravels

before our gaze

this one day
the space and face in us

that is all days

God's one day
that spacelessly invades us

This very God-gorgeous eternity
that always

irradiates us

7/1

## SNAIL OF LIGHT

Oh God Lord of who I am now
One God of all my inadequacies

lusts distractions blatherings recoils
recriminations thoughts — even sweet thoughts

imaginings

Won't You invade this shell that is me
with the Snail of Light that is Your

eternal purity
slower than no time

that I might rather live
timelessly in You

than in my self?

7/5

## LEVIATHAN'S SLEEP

A shell on the beach facing the sea's
rolling grasslands of salty light

where the moon cow munches from her
accustomed height

shedding rays on the watery turf
that ripples and bunches into fists

then flattens as if a deal's been made
with the surf's approval behind spattering mists

that hang in curtains above the plain below
with deeps so deep

nothing disturbs
Leviathan's sleep

7/11

# NIGHT AFTER NIGHT

The superlative explanations
caterpillars make as they

weave themselves into stasis and
total transformation

The tinge of gold around clouds as the
sun dips down or rises through silver skies

The dimple on a baby's cheek as she
smiles directly into your eyes for the

first time in half light

These divulgings of God's secret design made
manifest before our eyes

as the world like a fast bus
rushes past us into a yawning

gorge full of light deeper than
darkness and down

farther than depth

*and what do we conclude from it?*

What inferences do we make from
this or that telling gesture or shout in our

direction or direct or indirect question
that shivers us to the bone?

We raise a spoon from a
bowl to our lips

trusting its delight
and sip God's alchemical gold

in sip after sip

Light upon Light
day after day

night after night

                                                                        7/12

# HOW DO WE BREAK THE SHELL OPEN

How do we break the shell open
and if we break it open

will we see cosmos clearly
with God's true clarity in its true

flowing beams as He has
deemed it to be?

*Look!* Over there
dragons fighting for a morsel of meat

or *there!*
those dancers and singers suspended

as if by wings

All along the broken rim or
along the perfect smoothness

cosmos within cosmos —
but where do we begin?

A wild horse comes toward us
milder and milder the closer it gets

until it's standing before us
with a shake of its mane

and we mount it as it
vanishes from under us

We've slept on the cliff until we've
become the cliff

and merciful rain's fallen on the
no place we are

so only the cliff-face remains

and the horse rides off
to where the sun falls

into the sea
as we vanish

completely

7/13

## DEATH IS A PINHOLE

Death is a pinhole
the whole world goes through

Marching bands and flourishes
don't impede its progress

Death-masks and tragedy
don't mitigate its

absolute authority

Paint the pinhole as we will
the music from the other side

draws us on
in due time

along the great wall
that goes with us

as we go
onto which is projected

our lifelong
shadow show

Sing a song
or talk slow

each heartbeat reads out the one long
punctuated sentence

that melts away like
fresh snow

7/13

## HOLD ONTO THE LITTLE HANDLES

Hold onto the little handles on
either side of your soul

It's going to contain an ocean
with all its life there within it

and within that another ocean
and within each creature within it

yet another ocean within one deeper within it
until we're back where we started

looking out across it
pouring just the right amount into it

and just the right amount out of it
till all the cups are brimming with the

unutterable sweetness of your soul
and each shimmering surface has the

Prophet's face of the moon in it
and that moonlight is shed from it

in a timeless wink
simultaneously poured back into it

and filling it

## DOG TIRED

Dog tired I sit waiting for nothing
at the side of the bed

in the air all around and
all around everyone and every

living thing above ground
through which the most fantastic

plumaged beings plunge forward with
beady perfect eyes that so easily

size up prey from far away or how to
flit in between branches of trees

outside after the sun rises and
day begins

as anything and everything
swirls around us

including time and space in their
wedded calliope that hurries the

wooden horses around and around
God's central center that makes

a soft humming sound

7/17

## THE SUBLIME

The sublime at the fingernail of space
the mouth of night moving over the

stars

Trees who stretch to listen to distant
planetary drones across endlessness to

each other

And we hear all this without knowing it
We move in its mists and its

clarities

And most of all in eyeshine and hailstorm
air spray and lightness of touch

across miles of moments flickering their
delirious films

in tastes we swallow down mortal throats
as God singles us out for His Mercy

dot by dot

7/19

# WHEN THE DOOR SWINGS OPEN

When the door swings open
who do we see

in the eyes of the clouds?

What birdsong do we hear in the
top tree branches?

How does water flow so soothingly
as the planet we're on turns

in opposite directions?

*Oh hallowed be Thy Name!*

Unsounded except in every sound
Unseen except in every sight

Unthought and unthinkable except in every
unthinkable thought thought and still

thinking on

we proclaim you

Stairways come down to
catch us up

Fish stick their snouts out of water

Wings fill skies both seen and unseen
from earth to heaven

7/21

## ALWAYS PERFECT

To the already dead
*"We'll join you soon"*

in the time it takes to land
a man on the moon…

or one of the closer planets
and getting there in person

just as getting through death's door
in person

is such a rare and neat trick
we only do it once

and it's always perfect

7/24

## GOD'S GLANCE

Let all the books of wisdom I
haven't read or understood

coil inside this fragile shell of light
held up in the invisible

between me and infinite comprehension
kept somewhere inside me now

the way the ocean's kept inside its boundaries
and as deep in its own way as the sky in its

own way is endless

here in this present moment
tucked in the roof of the

mouth of my heart
in this only earthly existence I'll

ever know

with all its stretches
always out of reach

the way herds of giraffe gallop as
one across Serengeti's plains

or clouds mass and dissolve
above and all around us

in our planetary function

whose fundament is wisdom
and whose reality is

transparency
just as we are transparent

God's one glance
entering us from both sides

at once

7/24

## UNCREATED

Welcome into the volcanic chamber
This is where people remember

what they never knew they'd forgot

No fences here except of crystal
no trees except they burn like flames

and everywhere in the air float
angelic names

whose light explodes from a single dot

Stillness is enough to hear
what's drawn near to bring to bear

what's alive and scintillant everywhere
plucked out of thin air

But ground down to the rockiest point
and on our knees in a ball of flame

that yields up to us The Name
whose shudder resounds through it all

like an incandescent orb
held in the hand

A nothingness in the shape of a ball
that says it all

by containing a single grain of sand

Hold the heart there
in that last beat

abated

Hold to the land of heaven
the heavenly land

uncreated

                                                        7/25

## DOOR

Whoever has a door to walk through
should walk through it

If it's a trap door don't get
trapped in it

If it's a back door don't throw your
back out backing through it

But the best door is the door of the
floor you're standing on

the nowhere door that is everywhere
heart's door if you can find it

to walk through

looking out for the lions on the
other side who aren't there but

like to roar
through the door at you

down the long corridor —
*Oh forget about the long corridor*

just go straight through the door
as before

7/25

## WHERE WE SIT STILL

The toad who grew into a tree
The tree who grew into a globe

and hung suspended in a space of thought
one second after that and was

gone one second after that

The robe that swirled in vacant air
around a spirit light suspended

longer than thought
and hangs there still

and we are gone who watched it
grow

around the nothingness that wasn't
thrown round the nothingness that was

suspended as if

seated in a chair
where we sit still

7/29

## ALL THE PROPHETS

All the prophets on great lotuses
with their images reflected in vast

pools of sky upside-down to them
and the sky a sheet of silver stars

thrown against black turquoise
with a coppery fire burning behind it

and their voices melodiously entwining
in a mesh of bright music

each word as distinct as a
galaxy in its perfect space

busily revolving on its own vertical axis
as free-floating as thought or our

own origin plucked from seeming
nothingness to exist here for a time

before like corks on cascades we boil
over into the great sea of quiet

where you only hear these
prophets like drowned xylophones

beautifully intoning perfect sermons
for all creation to hear and

understand and put into practice
air by gulp of air and

beat by hammering heartbeat until the
world is done

8/1

## TO BE LOWERED DOWN

To be lowered down into a well of Light
past the scenes of our life

whose wavering trees hide in their shadows
the figures whose tissue is transparency

and whose voices are saying "farewell" with
every greeting

Lower and darker in our transcendent dive
deeper than ever before into this well

as concave as a tiger's open maw of
throat on fire and teeth

surrounding us

and as slim an escape past its
claws to the green valleys below

whose sunlight gilds everything that
blows or breathes

and whose halo surrounds our
beloved and his succession of progeny

flesh and blood and light upon light
sent by Allah's Merciful Glance

in the spacelessness before us
each moment of our descent

8/2

## IF IT'S A BUTTERFLY POEM YOU WANT

If it's a butterfly poem you want
flattering the air with its

flat-winged fluttering
cutting its own eccentric zigzags through

what's nothingness to it straight ahead and just onward
angle-flap by angle-flap

heading to nectar Oh sweet-hearted
companions of the wavering and

wavy way each wave-length a wingéd soul
message pulling us from our

deepmost green insideness in the
sweet jig-jag splendors of His

incandescent love

8/4

## NOT TILL

Not till you've been
torn out of the earth like the moon

can you understand the
diamond hardness of it

the light everywhere

Unspeakable
and nothing to be said

8/4

## ONE DROP IN A POOL

One drop in a pool
One pearl at the bottom of the sea

One sung note in the air
One planet in space

One space in all
One word suspended

incandescent with pulse

One pulse in the galaxies
supporting all

felt in our veins
as an unending river

emptying in a single drop
into a pool in space

at the bottom of the sea
caught in our veins

Endless note in the air
suspended and

singing in the radiant night

8/6

# WE ALL HAVE TO DIE

We all have to die
but we don't have to carry our

coffins around with us

We don't have to lie in them like
Rimbaud's mother

tossing and turning in the twisted sheets of a
hurricane of death

We don't have to ride the black
horse on the carousel

We can ride the white horse
galloping along a

white frothy shoreline

sight golden birds along our
arm's length at sundown

Walk as brisk as air walks
and take its twists and

turns it takes as we
walk in it as

fast as it walks

till we and it
can walk no more

but up to and through
the last door

                                                                  8/8

# A STRANGE HOLE IN OUR BEING

There's a strange hole in our being
that we would climb down into

all mossy and dark with
distant metallic or wooden wharf-like

echoes from either almost
too far away to hear or uncannily near that we can

just barely hear pronouncing or
almost pronouncing words of

solace and certainty and radiant
knowledges our consciousness doesn't

yet possess or seem to possess until we
somehow completely enter that

space through serious confinement and
preternatural and all-surrounding

darkness as measureless as all space itself
with us a turning orb in it a

planetary rock all craggy with secret
entranceways and a hole in it as well the

size of all the galaxies at once
beneficently presided over by their

Beneficent Creator who has not left us
comfortless nor ignorant slates devoid of

original writing in God's own electric
script comprehensible word by

lovingly articulated and roundly pronounced
word whose grammatical bodies actually

echo on the sides of this cavern that is
our selves and by stretching our

urgent hearing just enough
we can make out between heartbeats

and can then emerge with
the silencing enough of our own selves

to hear

8/9

# DOUBT

*"Je doute"* in French *"I doubt"*
*"Dudo"* in Spanish the same
I doubt if that word could have reached
such a pinnacle of fame

if Shaytan hadn't increased his whispering
between the spaces of what we see
to make us feel uneasy in this world
and shrink our vocabulary

that love should disappear
altogether from the equation
in regards to Divinity's care for us
in each earthly situation

If we cast all doubt away
and with it cast Shaytan
won't the world's light glitter blindingly
and its true freshness dawn?

8/10

## A SCATTERING OF ASHES

A scattering of ashes in the air
reminds us of our mortality

even if it's ashes of the world instead

floating into disappearance in an
air that also disappears

and the soul is the only pivot that remains
gazing at it from where it

stands or sits

and God remains the only pivot within that
pivot both before and after

and the world's ashes blow like breath
through an empty eye

as our soul's breath
only blows from God

Face to face
and eye to eye

8/10

## THE FAMILY OF MAN

In the Family of Man as it's been called
are some saints and some idiots

and by idiots I mean those
whack jobs who think they

own the universe and can do as they please

and then there are sheep and ants and
carnivores of various sizes and

stripes and grass eaters of various
sincerities and hypocrisies

nibbling away at our credulity

And God has blessed them all equally
but He's poured something uncanny

like a liquid gold or silver into the
saints among us

who seem to be speaking and acting
from a different space altogether

from the rest of us with our
sniveling and complaints

They walk out of a car crash
clapping their hands

sing at the center and at the periphery
at the same time

seem to run as fast as the cougar
in what they can do in such a

short time covering ground in
seconds that takes the rest of us

years

And then there's the idiots who make
all the rest of us even the

saints look bad causing utter
destruction and mayhem toppling

sacred buildings and bulldozing the
poor and indigent spoiling

everything for the rest of us out of their
unstoppable annoyance in their

two-dimensional universe of things

So that as flowers grow and fade
and sidewalks crack

let's hope we stay near saintly company
since these are all inside us

rattling like nails in a can
and God give us strength to see past

the firewall to where coolness prevails
in snow time or scorch time

The perfectly formed leaf
and the drop of light that

illuminates it
and our hearts able to

appreciate its meaning
in the stillest of centers

8/12

## NOT SO FAST!

*"Not so fast!"*
said the parent to the child

or maybe it was death
talking to life

An ox stands up to its knees
in a rice paddy

Isn't that enough?

*"Don't be stupid"*
said a butterfly to a bee

or maybe it was a car crash
about to occur

and the bee also
went along anyway

each to his own honey

8/14

# THE PARTICULARS OF ANY GIVEN THING

The particulars of any given thing

you know
twenty shimmering wings on each side

a thousand interchanging faces
rippling upward each second

that give a thing its particular flavor

How light from multiple sources at
once gives the flying a look of

incessant corkscrew motion in space say
or a wash-like gushing flow as of

cascades of dappled water

ceaselessly moving in all directions
from multiple centers to

endless circumferences accompanied by

an ethereal sound that comes from
everywhere in space and soothes the

heart that not since
childhood has been so thoroughly soothed

that kind of thing

And then the suspension of it all
above rainbow-plenty canyons themselves

brilliantly multicolored in ever-changing
sunlight but from another

sun than earthly sunshine in its
velvety texture and tinfoil shimmer

playing ceaselessly across it all

and somehow illuminating our
own faces and bodies also suspended

at the same level that seems to be

gradually upwardly diving in a kind of
watery slow-motion

as planetary valleys and peaks pass
below us themselves dissolving into

soft oceanic maelstroms in
constant inward motion

for example
and all this in crystal-clear transparency

calling out the name of Allah from

every pore of itself and echoed by

every pore of ours in ascending choirs
whose sound is a flashed glory of shivering

spectrums tasty to the tongue
like something more delicious than

anything tasted before

and all of this more
wide awake than ever

for instance
forever

and this only the
beginning

this only a
hint of it

8/17

# THE CORKSCREWING MOTION

The corkscrewing motion of the entire
universe by which I mean

every billion galaxy cluster as we
zoom in every direction each one

light years away from any in its
close neighborhood with by what we

know by telescope vast emptiness in between
but which no doubt contains

just as many in between perhaps as the
entire collection in space contains

or multiples of that and more
the whole made one twist by Allah on a

tabletop in one of His lit domains
like a toy top in amusing circular swiftness

in a room of infinite tabletops each with a
similar collection of galaxies with no

possible conceivable number to any of this
against a lovely starry background

as velvety as a kitten's throat hairs
Allah's love what turns them all

the most potent unquantifiable energy
compelling each possible motion

and all of that in a thimble-sized
container of light bursting in its

ocean of darkness in trillion similar thimbles
none of which what they seem

*O impossible considerations* that
soften our hearts in front of

everything we know and everything we
can't know which has

everything we know swimming in one
blink of His breath as He

gazes on it in the unspatial where
His nowhereness

perfectly and contently isn'tly
is

8/18

## THE GREAT BEAR'S BACK

The great bear's back
and the fine lion's mane
and the peacock's strut
and the eagle's float

make us see back in time
to a world almost gone
except in the populous heart
that holds worlds in full array

until we've all gone down
where ants and worms confide
their best kept secrets to earth
where we'll all dwell at last

in the river of light below
the rivers bears relish
in a roar of silence louder
than any lion's roar

and a display of iridescence
more dazzling than peacock flash
sailing in our soul's first space
that humbles an eagle's pride

8/20

# WHEN THE SUBJECT IS LOVE

When the subject is love
a hundred transparent angels rush in all our

doors at once
each containing a billion transparent angels holding

blue lit candles

Wheels of sparks in space the size of mountains
teams of invisible horses as numerous as

stars come down from the hills

When the subject is love
all the cards in the gambling hall turn to Aces

Even the flames in a burning house
become kisses

It's madness and mayhem of the
loveliest kind in a

cool veneer

Sailors in a sinking ship
start swimming like eels to

dry land or a thriving Atlantis undersea

Spoons cutting into melons
come away with a cream more

delicious than nectar from
Scandinavian mythologies

Each of our words comes equipped
with an orchestra of light

Every bridge we cross is flung over
Paradise rivers

The whirring of wings we hear
is not just hummingbirds

lighter than thoughts departing from
worry into perpetual sunrise

When the subject is love
saints are on hand with raised glasses

and starlight gleams from their wine
glistening the edges of a circular globe

Texts appear in the air at eye level
each sentence more spectacular than the

last with white stags and does leaping between all the
nouns and verbs with that

look in their eyes old romances describe

become now utterly indescribable

As each wingéd doorway opens around us in space
we find ourselves flowing through

like water seeking its level
in a turquoise sea

and we witness horizons more
inside us than before us

the cosmos pouring through us with all its
sizzling crickets more than

noisily around us now with distance and
mystery unfurled into

immediate wonder

honey on the tongue

night made spherical with

radiant voices

8/22

# I SHOULD SLEEP

I should sleep
but one star keeps nudging me awake

Winds blow on that star
raising silver flakes of dust that

contort into vivid sacred sentences before
settling down

slithering along the star's dark surface like a
low flying carpet

Does this distant beam keep me
awake just now or something

so deep inside the heart it
links up to the sunken baths of

Bethesda the dripping pools where
Jesus stepped and bathed in

daylight's darkness?

What drove me to write this
when I should turn in to sleep

and the ants and antlers of the
world are restlessly moving through space

in all the perfection of their pursuits
going from God to God again

knowing somewhere in our souls
He's both transit and goal

origin and end
each breath a free flight into

round window-ledges of radiance

                                                8/24

## IF I LAY MY HEAD

If I lay my head against this
hive of a pillow

will the Unseen world reveal its
secrets to me?

Can I get to it through here?
What's this consciousness God's

given us —
horse training and dog shows?

Dark hedges full of snakes?
Rings of fire and flaming hoops of gold?

If I lie straight and close my eyes
will I drop down into it as

into a coffin whose transparent sides
give me a good glimpse of Paradise?

You've sent us here fully equipped that's
for sure

Else why populate Your earth if we're not
working astrolabes of perfect navigation?

Won't silence tell me more than
all my chatter?

The zebras all look at us straight on
from their clown zigzags black on

white or vice-versa

I'm seeing endless rolling greenery now
in hills and dales

disappearing in the sundown distance

God Who presides so
cunningly and near

bend close on us sleepers with Your
nightly kiss

and let us wake with its imprint
like honey on our lips

8/29

## LAMBS AND LIONS

Are lambs that ask the way to heaven
the same as lions?

One has eyes that never leave the ground
the other's head's held high in the sky's bright sunlight

One quiet as a mouse and soft as a cloud
the other's mane like fire and teeth like death's

Do they trod the earth the same and
leave the same trail behind them?

When lambs roar they make a
stuttering sound

If a lion's meek it may be it's on its
last legs

Where our eyes land is what our
hearts desire

For big things go for gold
for small things watch leaves

blow past the windows and be gone

The screen's blank and everything passes
past it

But neither screen nor passing thoughts have
substantiality

Lions and lambs both land in
God's land at last

enwrapped together in the circle of His love

Baaing and roaring become
perfect murmurs

all eternity long

9/4

## POEM FOUND ON A SCRAP OF PAPER AND RECONSIDERED

I was remembering myself
now seventy-three

at three or seven
but more like seven

left on my own
while mom and dad went out on the town

and feeling both sad and so alone
that I began at that age

to get things done

like drawing or dreaming
listening to the radio

or doing all three
on my fantasy patio

# FROM THE SOFT ROPE WE ARE

From the soft rope we are
from the jagged tear in a canvas we are

from the wrecked and twisted bicycle we are
from the lengthy shadow of a lost world we are

from flickers at the edge of a dark wood we are
from an echoing empty stadium at midnight we are

from crumbs left for birds on a windowsill we are
from the signal sent from a ship's fo'c'sle we are

From land sighted and land ignored we are
from polished silver laid out perfectly we are

From a peak wreathed in roseate cloud we are
from a low-lying hamlet under brown smoke we are

From rows of burgeoning grape-trellises we are
from a sunny valley between green hills we are

From the spontaneous defenses of our sovereignty we are
from silence in the midst of chaos we are

From dust flakes falling down an endless chute we are
from an abrupt announcement at the table we are

From a door slammed and a door left open we are
From blue fog suddenly filling a deep canyon we are

From no one left in the meeting hall but us we are
from just one more face in the billowing crowd we are

From oft-blessed in abundance from we know not where we are
from bereft never knowingly visited by angels we are

From fervent supplications each dawn religiously we are
from the last whispered breath of prayer when we die we are

when even stillness stands still
right where we are

O God in Your Magnificence and Glory
Who moves us and moves in us

without Whom we would not be
whoever and wherever we are

Bring out from us what light You will
and quench us with every breath

in Your only existence
when no more than a shadow of a shadow of a shadow we are

Small flickering light in Your window we are
tiny birdsong of distant jubilant whistling

heard near and far
we are

9/5

# DEATH DELIGHTS IN OUR AMOROUS PLAY

Death delights in our amorous play
and wouldn't have it any other way

That we kiss its face with our woolly lips
and our eyes grow drunk at its sweet eclipse

That we stand stock still as it shivers over us
in the middle of our road where it's discovered us

With our ten more words of whispered love
that fit tightly round us like a velvet glove

That we gaze at the place it wishes to take us
and go there without it having to make us

It loves that we love it so exclusively
in a moment that arrives so elusively

Here's our true love who won't betray us
though it slay us

# THE SOUND OF GRASS GROWING

1

The sound of grass growing
and of the planet spinning through space

*that sound!*

Of the tiny ticks in inches expanding
and all things in their own living souls

stirring as they come awake or
wriggle in their sleep inside God's

starry blanket

each star of which and each galaxy of which
makes that sound!

Sung now by the train in West Drayton
clacking its tracks a few streets away

and the roar of silence surrounding it
and first bird chortle not far

away as the train clack lessens and the
space roar gets louder

each raindrop marimba clonging

*that sound!*

Each rush of it in our veins
toward its original ocean

opening its throat
in God-space never silent and never

anything but echoing
*that sound!*


2

The roaring of tiniest things
falling through space

roaring with manifest Presence

happily floating
with His audible and inaudible

melodious monolog each fleck or flake makes
into and out of us

and those bacterial squirts in our
stomachs at night those juices in their

amazing passages keeping us
alive in His roaring Word

all conducted by the great
avalanche orchestra of time

come and gone and ever present
never come never gone and always

ever present
His timeless

roaring Word

head back and howling
through us all

9/15

# FROM OUR POINT OF VIEW

From our point of view
we're the only ones alive

All living things circulate
around us

obvious to our central and
centrifugal perceptions

All sparrows in their flight
tending toward us or

away from us

When we open our mouths
sparrows don't fly out of them

in their intentional trajectories
but they fill a tree over there

and fly from *there*
to *there* outside us

their sparrow eyes seeing as
much for them as they need

to fulfill their wide "sparrowness"

We hike to see waterfalls
and listen to their colossal

crunch of water down rocks

Even bacteria inside us
are outside our scope

as we're the living ones and
they're inside us

But if Allah is The Living One
and each wise squirrel or

rhinoceros could speak
theologically about His

sovereign light

some deep insight would be
shed on things instead of just

pictures in a book for our
amusement

as they afterwards turn to
go to continue their lives

carrying nuts to a good
hiding place or

squinting rhinocerosly through tall grass

And the many living oceans that we
are continue washing round

His shore His central hub His true and single
Self-Awareness

which we mirror as moonily
as we can with all our

lunatic energies
each of us singing our own song

that echoes against the sky
like silver light radiating back

from a flung reflection

squirrel song as strong
and rhinoceros hum

as sweetly sung

each single living conscious note
an entire song

9/17

## GRIZZLY PANTOMIME

Through the cold and drizzly night
a giant troupe of clumsy grizzly bears

performs a pantomime

They swat each other and
bonk each other over their heads with

clubs

They put on human masks and mock
our foibles

They roll over forwards and fall
backwards to make the audience laugh

One plays dead and with grizzly
solemnity

they perform a funeral
hunching their shoulders in grief

dabbing those little black eyes of theirs
with hairy claws

their black curly nails wiping away
crocodile tears

Then the dead bear bounces back to
life and they whizz around on

tricycles looking oafish honking little
horns and howling

In the depths of the night in a deep dark
glade this troupe of bears

acts out our
mortal moments casting huge

jagged shadows against surrounding
tree trunks from lanterns they

swing around one by one of them
as they one by one now lumber off

into the deep dark wood from
which they came blowing little

brass trumpets and ringing little glass bells
and silence falls again

as their growls trail off
into the black black night

and are gone

9/19

## NEARSIGHTEDNESS

In my nearsightedness

around the full moon

a rainbow nimbus

9/20
(in the backyard in Yiewsley, West Drayton, Greater London, UK)

# ENTER FROM THE RIGHT

Enter from the right
but not too far right

In fact enter from the center
*just appear*

Everything enters from the center
neither left nor right

neither background nor foreground
*just appears*

appears to emerge forward

nether backward nor forward
reveals itself in God's bliss

element after element from its own self bared
by His *fiat* so eloquently made

comes at us as we at it
when it and we

meet as we meet

in that self-same center
at His sweet will

neither good nor ill
everything from its center

in its own

stillness

> 9/23
> (in the air over the Atlantic)

## WHEN AN ANGEL PASSES BY YOUR DOOR

When an angel passes by your door
polished wood will glow and
apples tumble

If an angel enters
the room will swirl and pastures bloom
thin rays of purplish gold threads
flecked among the pasturage

When one sits next to you as
one is sitting now
nothing passes you by but that its
demeanor burnished to a higher shine
emits a liveliness always there
but not always as witnessed

When an angel's gone on to others
as all angels do
the sky's silver tinges seem to deepen
and all dimensions go back and

back indicating more than we
thought was there
and that there's much more here to here
than we thought before

9/24

## DEATH SITS IN ALL OUR WINDOWS

Death sits in all our windows
in a green apron

smiling at us with a variable face

How are we going to greet its smile
if our zebras aren't tamed

and our lions still lunge at the bars
startling the onlookers?

The trees around us are so dense only a
thin green light seeps through

yet our darknesses aren't really
dark enough for us to see clearly

Death shifts position from window to window
but it's always the same

window for all of us

and even the sweet sailing ships in the
nearest harbor with their

yellow streamers and rainbow
sails flapping in blue sunlight

have a compromised captain and one
map that goes to

only one destination

Out of the winds that
move all things

a calm voice with
tympani depth and piccolo resonance

comes clear to our ears
whose listening heart's

black windows shiver
with sudden starlight

we can walk out through
in one part harmony

9/26

## DRAWN TO THE PRESENCE

Drawn to the Presence by a
single bead of light

through the eye of a needle that is
everything but God

in this world held in the clutched
embrace of the next

surrounded by the incessant march of
nothingness

in gaudy dress
to an insane music

that in reality is stone silence gazing out on
silent sands

hushed in magnificence

9/28

BUBBLES

Soap bubbles come from Mars I'm
told on good authority

my source kept mum

Like the exoskeletons of bugs bubbles
are all that remain of their

thriving civilizations

thin filmy spheres
gone in a second but lovely in the

light light's spectrum can

beautify playing over their
rondures on the way out

now a planet of rusty dust and
dunes once an emerald city of

ephemeral splendor
resided inside by spherical beings with

unpronounceable names that to
us sounds like all consonants

but to them was music to their ears
somehow built into the

surface of their spheres

harmonica-like sounds circulating through
the Martian air

linking castle to castle across the
continents

now fluffy bubbles in our baths and
dish water —

*makes you want to weep*

10/2

## BEAUTY IN THE BREATH

The beauty in the breath and in the
golden breast

as it floats out across a mirror lake
with herons calligraphing the

air into elegant messages
indecipherable to our minds but as

clear as a clown's eye to the heart

when the clown's a mix of
poignancy and foolishness in floppy

gestures and perfect strokes before
scampering away

The beauty that the redwoods display as they
fan sunbeams down from their

high branches onto the forest floor
as if great sky wheels were

majestically turning down
thin enormous trunks to their feet

Unnamable beauty that
pops in the air the moment we see it

and radiates throughout our bodies
as we remain upright

in a still and single spot

                                                                10/3

# IN HONOR OF ALL THE POETS

In honor of all the poets who will
die one day

leaving hair in their hairbrushes
and teeth marks on whatever it is

they bit down on

No path over a sunny hill blazing with
radiance is too sweet for them as they

salute horses heads down in clover
and multiple combinations of

clouds massing and unmassing
above them

They've been everywhere already and
even somewheres only their

cries and chants can go
taking any takers with them

who can take it and who can
take the chance

*Here's to them!*
left at the wayside

crying like lepers
losing every bodily characteristic

in God's greater wind

singing through it all
nothing left at last

but disembodied voices
in Egyptian wilderness

in Nordic sunset

white against white

*the soul's home*

10/4

# HE'S LEFT THIS WORLD

He's left this world pretty
much as he found it except

he'd been here
and that salient and ineradicable

fact is all the difference and
why some of the atoms in one place where he

arrived on the scene are now in
another place and an untold

merry-go-round of souls that crossed
paths with his in

varying amounts of intimacy
are not exactly the

same as if he'd not been here at all

and some birds in trees sing
higher or louder or softer

because he was here

and some creeks running through
dark and tangly woods

run more glisteningly or more
melodiously because one day he

walked alongside them whistling an
unforgettable tune to their waters who

repeat and repeat the
pattern of his song whale-like

until even the surrounding
wildlife also falls a bit under its

spell and some squirrels might

wait for a minute the way
squirrels do standing on their

haunches to listen to his tune
before moving on

and some birds might catch onto it
and even teach it to their young

10/5

# IN A WELL

In a well just one step inside us
down in whose darkness

a perfect raw diamond shines

At a windowsill where your
many arms have rested

looking out at nothing or a string of
hills or flakes or sunlight

and seeing God's Face
in each place first

Down  a strange trail in a woods
that feels as if lined by elves

and may be in invisibility
blending in daylight by day

and night by night

and the corner of subtle
planetary motions

and the pupil of the vision of depth
in the clouds or above the clouds

that surrounds everything

and the light it sheds like cat hairs
on everything

is the soul's home
perfectly fitting and fitted

each seam perfectly in place
never blown apart nor

tsunami-trounced

with an easy smile on its face
seeing nothing

but His

radiant Face

10/7

## VELVET GLOVE

I feel in my body
like I'm inside a

velvet glove

10/7

## FILLED TO OVERFLOWING

Filled to overflowing
the eye of a small chickadee

or human

a gnat flying
in God's world

The expansive panorama
wrapped around us

its measureless oceans
surrounding us

one star alone enough to
fill us

but entire galaxies
pouring through us

a single stable standing here
under its canopy

situation in time
making time in a

timeless presence

That lie having said it
dissolved in

starlight
catching the scent of

faraway places
God everywhere at once

in His palpable nowhereness
tip of a finger

on the rim of a glass
finger laid aside of a

nose in a
whisper of thought

*Where are we in all this?*

Lost in it

hailstones of nothingness
rock-hard resiliency

soft as ice melting in
mid-space

catastrophe contained in a
breath

breath lofted in
flow

so fine its
fineness

denied and sent
flying

home

10/8

# INDEX

A Long Session of Non Sequiturs   103
A Million Birds   16
A Scattering of Ashes   166
A Strange Hole in Our Being   163
A Sunset   42
All the Prophets   154
Along the Way   61
Always Perfect   147
Answer Enough   130
At the Square Edge   97
Author's Introduction   10
Beauty in the Breath   207
Bubbles   205
Death Delights in Our Amorous Play   189
Death is a Pinhole   140
Death Sits in All Our Windows   202
Dog Tired   143
Door   152
Doubt   165
Drawn to the Presence   204
Enter from the Right   199
Equipoise   78
Filled to Overflowing   216
From Our Point of View   193
From the Soft Rope We Are   187
Get Up Out of Sound Sleep   128
God's Glance   148
God's One Day   132
Grizzly Pantomime   196
He's Left This World   211
Heart to Heart   19
Hold onto the Little Handles   142
Holy Spots   20

Horses of Fajr    69
How Do We Break the Shell Open    138
I Float in a Sea    100
I Get Ready for Sleep    101
I Should Sleep    180
If I Lay My Head    182
If I Turned into Death    95
If it's a Butterfly Poem You Want    158
In a Well    213
In Honor of All the Poets    209
In Switzerland    44
Is That His Love?    121
Its Silver Threads    115
Lambs and Lions    184
Last Day    85
Leviathan's Sleep    135
Lightning Bolts    24
Lotus in Reverse    92
Naked Before My Cat    89
Nearsightedness    198
Night After Night    136
Not So Fast!    170
Not Till    159
One Drop in a Pool    160
Paradise of Buzzes    106
Perspicacious    40
Poem Found on a Scrap of Paper and Reconsidered    186
Prostration    43
Silver Ladder    66
Since When Did the World    110
Single Pointed    71
Snail of Light    134
Somebody's Knocking    76
Something    81
Songs of Our Souls    32

The Certain Gaze the Sky Has    111
The Corkscrewing Motion    174
The Day Comes    70
The Family of Man    167
The Great Bear's Back    176
The Joys of a Breath    35
The Particulars of Any Given Thing    171
The Path    26
The Puzzle    37
The Savage in the Lamplight    117
The Sound of Grass Growing    190
The Sublime    144
The Waters of Night    64
The Weight of The World    67
The World Looks Very Different    22
They Let Me Down Slowly    63
They Say    124
Three Pilgrims    13
Time Goes So Fast    113
To Be Lowered Down    156
To Reach the Water    83
Touchstone    74
Uncreated    150
Vanishing Horizon    87
Velvet Glove    215
Waking Up in the Same Room    119
Water That Trickles    105
We All Have to Die    161
We Could Dry Up    94
What is Lost    107
When an Angel Passes by Your Door    201
When the Door Swings Open    145
When the Subject is Love    177
Where the Greatest Wisdom Is    90
Where We Sit Still    153

## ABOUT THE AUTHOR

Born in 1940 in Oakland, California, Daniel Abdal-Hayy Moore had his first book of poems, *Dawn Visions*, published by Lawrence Ferlinghetti of City Lights Books, San Francisco, in 1964, and the second in 1972, *Burnt Heart/Ode to the War Dead*. He created and directed *The Floating Lotus Magic Opera Company* in Berkeley, California in the late 60s, and presented two major productions, *The Walls Are Running Blood*, and *Bliss Apocalypse*. He became a Sufi Muslim in 1970, performed the Hajj in 1972, and lived and traveled throughout Morocco, Spain, Algeria and Nigeria, landing in California and publishing *The Desert is the Only Way Out*, and *Chronicles of Akhira* in the early 80s (Zilzal Press). Residing in Philadelphia since 1990, in 1996 he published *The Ramadan Sonnets* (Jusoor/City Lights), and in 2002, *The Blind Beekeeper* (Jusoor/Syracuse University Press). He has been the major editor for a number of works, including *The Burdah* of Shaykh Busiri, translated by Hamza Yusuf, and the poetry of Palestinian poet, Mahmoud Darwish, translated by Munir Akash. He is also widely published on the worldwide web: *The American Muslim, DeenPort*, and his own website and poetry blog, among others: *www.danielmoorepoetry.com, www.ecstaticxchange.wordpress.com*. He has been poetry editor for *Seasons Journal, Islamica Magazine,* a 2010 translation by Munir Akash of *State of Siege*, by Mahmoud Darwish (Syracuse University Press), and *The Prayer of the Oppressed*, by Imam Muhammad Nasir al-Dar'i, translated by Hamza Yusuf. In 2011, 2012 and 2014 he was a winner of the Nazim Hikmet Prize for Poetry. In 2013 he won an American Book Award, and was listed among The 500 Most Influential Muslims for his poetry. *The Ecstatic Exchange Series* is bringing out the extensive body of his works of poetry (a complete list of published works on page 2).

# POETIC WORKS by Daniel Abdal-Hayy Moore
Published and Unpublished

Dawn Visions (published by City Lights, 1964)
Burnt Heart/Ode to the War Dead (published by City Lights, 1972)
This Body of Black Light Gone Through the Diamond (printed by Fred Stone, Cambridge, Mass, 1965)
On The Streets at Night Alone (1965?)
All Hail the Surgical Lamp (1967)
States of Amazement (1970)

---

Abdallah Jones and the Disappearing-Dust Caper (published by The Ecstatic Exchange/Crescent Series, 2006)
'Ala ud-Deen and the Magic Lamp (published by The Ecstatic Exchange, 2011)
The Chronicles of Akhira (1981) (published by Zilzal Press with Typoglyphs by Karl Kempton, 1986; published in Sparrow on the Prophet's Tomb by The Ecstatic Exchange, 2009)
Mouloud (1984) (A Zilzal Press chapbook, 1995; published in Sparrow on the Prophet's Tomb by The Ecstatic Exchange, 2009)
The Crown of Creation (1984) (published by The Ecstatic Exchange, 2012)
The Look of the Lion (The Parabolas of Sight) (1984)
The Desert is the Only Way Out (completed 4/21/84) (Zilzal Press chapbook, 1985)
Atomic Dance (1984) (am here books, 1988)
Outlandish Tales (1984)
Awake as Never Before (12/26/84) (Zilzal Press chapbook, 1993)
Glorious Intervals (1/1/85) (Zilzal Press chapbook, ?)
Long Days on Earth/Book I (1/28 – 8/30/85)
Long Days on Earth/Book II (Hayy Ibn Yaqzan)
Long Days on Earth/Book III (1/22/86)
Long Days on Earth/Book IV (1986)
The Ramadan Sonnets (Long Days on Earth/Book V) (5/9 – 6/11/86) (published by Jusoor/City Lights Books, 1996) (republished as Ramadan Sonnets by The Ecstatic Exchange, 2005)
Long Days on Earth/Book VI (6-8/30/86)
Holograms (9/4/86 – 3/26/87)
History of the World (The Epic of Man's Survival) (4/7 – 6/18/87)
Exploratory Odes (6/25 – 10/18/87)

The Man at the End of the World (11/11 – 12/10/87)
The Perfect Orchestra (3/30 – 7/25/88)(published by The Ecstatic Exchange, 2009)
Fed from Underground Springs (7/30 – 11/23/88)
Ideas of the Heart (11/27/88 – 5/5/89)
New Poems (scattered poems, out of series, from 3/24 – 8/9/89)
Facing Mecca (5/16 – 11/11/89)
A Maddening Disregard for the Passage of Time (11/17/89 – 5/20/90) (published by The Ecstatic Exchange, 2009)
The Heart Falls in Love with Visions of Perfection (6/15/90 – 6/2/91)
Like When You Wave at a Train and the Train Hoots Back at You (Farid's Book) (6/11 – 7/26/91) (published by The Ecstatic Exchange, 2008)
Orpheus Meets Morpheus (8/1/91 – 3/14/92)
The Puzzle (3/21/92 – 8/17/93)(published by The Ecstatic Exchange, 2011)
The Greater Vehicle (10/17/93 – 4/30/94)
A Hundred Little 3-D Pictures (5/14/94 – 9/11/95) (published by The Ecstatic Exchange, 2013)
The Angel Broadcast (9/29 – 12/17/95)
Mecca/Medina Time-Warp (12/19/95 – 1/6/96) (published as a Zilzal Press chapbook, 1996)(published in Sparrow on the Prophet's Tomb, 2009)
Miracle Songs for the Millennium (1/20 – 10/16/96)(published by The Ecstatic Exchange, 2014)
The Blind Beekeeper (11/15/96 – 5/30/97) (published 2002 by Jusoor/Syracuse University Press)
Chants for the Beauty Feast (6/3 – 10/28/97)(published by The Ecstatic Exchange, 2011
You Open a Door and it's a Starry Night (10/29/97 – 5/23/98) (published by The Ecstatic Exchange, 2009)
Salt Prayers (5/29 – 10/24/98) (published by The Ecstatic Exchange, 2005)
Some (10/25/98 – 4/25/99)
Flight to Egypt (5/1 – 5/16/99)
I Imagine a Lion (5/21 – 11/15/99) (published by The Ecstatic Exchange, 2006)
Millennial Prognostications (11/25/99 – 2/2/2000) (published by the Ecstatic Exchange, 2009)
Shaking the Quicksilver Pool (2/4 – 10/8/2000) (published by The Ecstatic Exchange, 2009)
Blood Songs (10/9/2000 – 4/3/2001)(Published by The Ecstatic Exchange,

2012)

The Music Space (4/10 – 9/16/2001) (published by The Ecstatic Exchange, 2007)
Where Death Goes (9/20/2001 – 5/1/2002) (published by The Ecstatic Exchange, 2009)
The Flame of Transformation Turns to Light (99 Ghazals Written in English) (5/14 – 8/21/2002) (published by The Ecstatic Exchange, 2007)
Through Rose-Colored Glasses (7/22/2002 – 1/15/2003) (published by The Ecstatic Exchange, 2007)
Psalms for the Broken-Hearted (1/22 – 5/25/2003) (published by The Ecstatic Exchange, 2006)
Hoopoe's Argument (5/27 – 9/18/03)
Love is a Letter Burning in a High Wind (9/21 – 11/6/2003) (published by The Ecstatic Exchange, 2006)
Laughing Buddha/Weeping Sufi (11/7/2003 – 1/10/2004) (published by The Ecstatic Exchange, 2005)
Mars and Beyond (1/20 – 3/29/2004) (published by The Ecstatic Exchange, 2005)
Underwater Galaxies (4/5 – 7/21/2004) (published by The Ecstatic Exchange, 2007)
Cooked Oranges (7/23/2004 – 1/24/2005 (published by The Ecstatic Exchange, 2007)
Holiday from the Perfect Crime (1/25 – 6/11/2005)(published by The Ecstatic Exchange, 2011)
Stories Too Fiery to Sing Too Watery to Whisper (6/13 – 10/24/2005)
Coattails of the Saint (10/26/2005 – 5/10/2006 ) (published by The Ecstatic Exchange, 2006)
In the Realm of Neither (5/14/2006 – 11/12/06) (published by The Ecstatic Exchange, 2008)
Invention of the Wheel (11/13/06 – 6/10/07)(published by The Ecstatic Exchange, 2010)
The Sound of Geese Over the House (6/15 – 11/4/07)
The Fire Eater's Lunchbreak (11/11/07 – 5/19/2008) (published by The Ecstatic Exchange, 2008)
Sparks Off the Main Strike (5/24/2008 – 1/10/2009)(published by The Ecstatic Exchange, 2010)
Stretched Out on Amethysts (1/13 – 9/17/2009)(published by The Ecstatic

Exchange, 2010)
The Throne Perpendicular to All that is Horizontal (9/18/09 – 1/25/10)
In Constant Incandescence (2/10 – 8/13/10) (published by The Ecstatic Exchange, 2011)
The Caged Bear Spies the Angel (8/30/10 – 3/6/11)(published by The Ecstatic Exchange, 2010)
This Light Slants Upward (3/7 – 10/13/11)
Ramadan is Burnished Sunlight (part of This Light Slants Upward, published separately by The Ecstatic Exchange, 2011)
The Match That Becomes a Conflagration (10/14/11 – 5/9/12)
Down at the Deep End (5/10 – 8/3/12) (published by The Ecstatic Exchange, 2012)
Next Life (8/9/12 – 2/12/13) (published by The Ecstatic Exchange, 2013)
The Soul's Home (2/13 – 10/8/13) (published by The Ecstatic Exchange, 2014)
Eternity Shimmers & Time Holds its Breath (10/10/13 – 1/27/14)
He Comes Running (part of Eternity Shimmers, published as an Ecstatic Exchange Chapbook, 2014)
The Sweet Enigma of it All (1/28/14 – )

www.ingramcontent.com/pod-product-compliance
Lightning Source LLC
Chambersburg PA
CBHW032042150426
43194CB00006B/383